EASY PIANO

Big Band

Arranged by Bernadine Johnson

M000087255

CONTENTS

Produced by
Alfred Music Publishing Co., Inc.
P.O. Box 10003
Van Nuys, CA 91410-0003
alfred.com

Printed in USA.

ISBN-10: 0-7390-7330-3
ISBN-13: 978-0-7390-7330-8

 Alfred Cares. Contents printed on 100% recycled paper.

DON'T SIT UNDER THE APPLE TREE

(With Anyone Else But Me)

Words and Music by
Charlie Tobias, Lew Brown and Sam H. Stept
Arranged by Bernadine Johnson

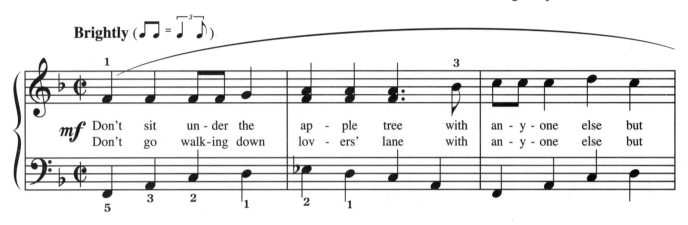

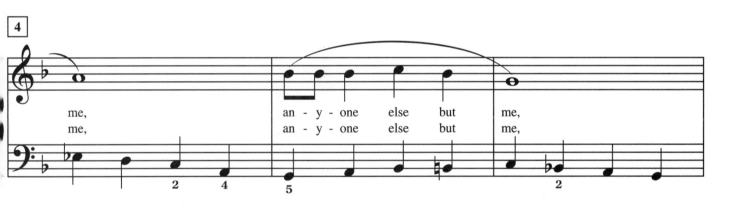

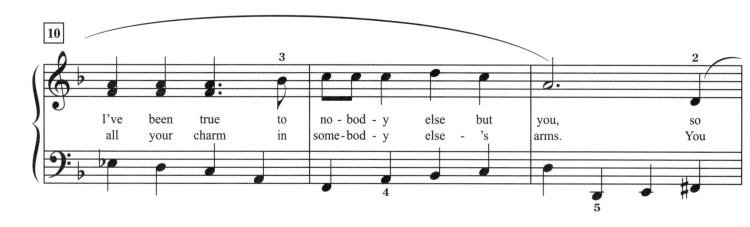

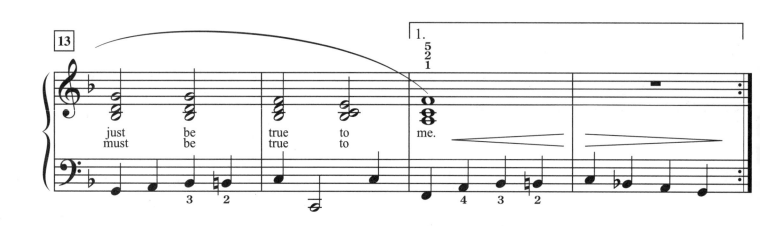

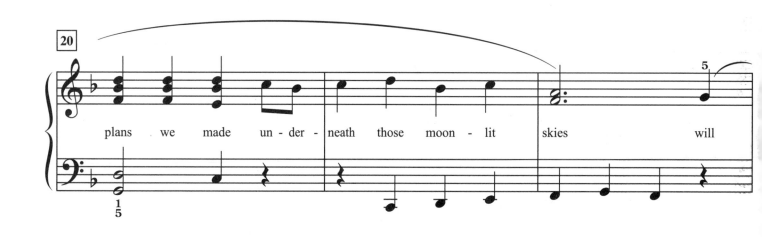

CHATTANOOGA CHOO CHOO

Music by Harry Warren
Lyrics by Mack Gordon
Arranged by Bernadine Johnson

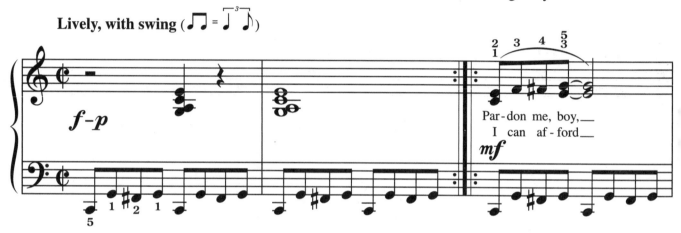

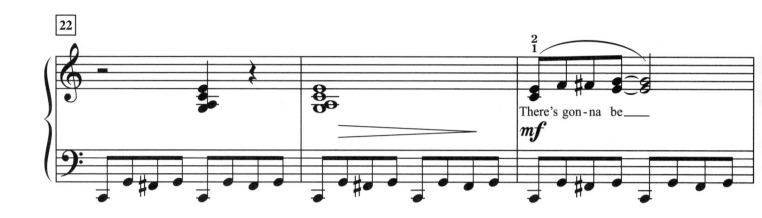

There's gon-na be____

_mf_

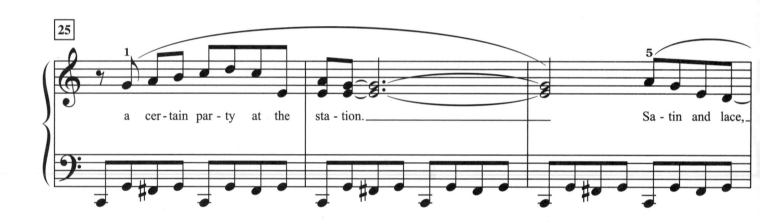

a cer-tain par-ty at the sta-tion.____ Sa-tin and lace,

I used to call "Fun-ny Face."

She's gon - na cry___ un - til I tell her that I'll

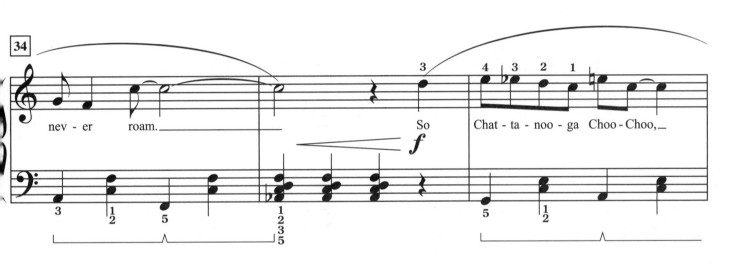

nev - er roam.___ ___ So Chat - ta - noo - ga Choo - Choo,___

won't you choo - choo me home.

IT DON'T MEAN A THING

(If It Ain't Got That Swing)

Music by Duke Ellington
Words by Irving Mills
Arranged by Bernadine Johnson

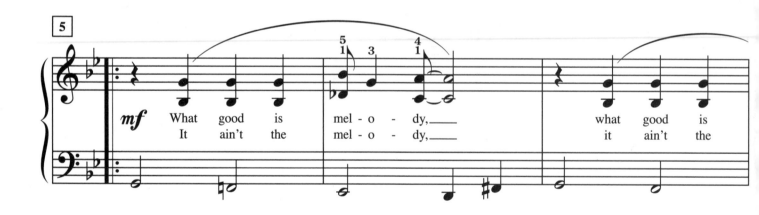

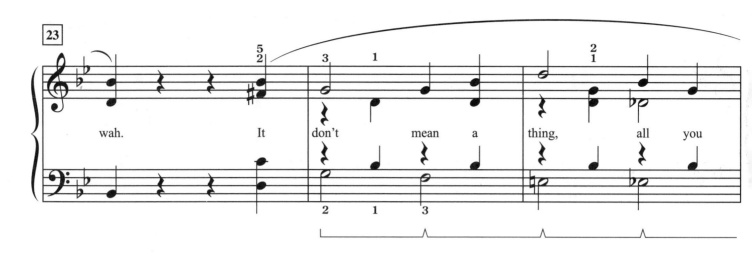

wah. It don't mean a thing, all you

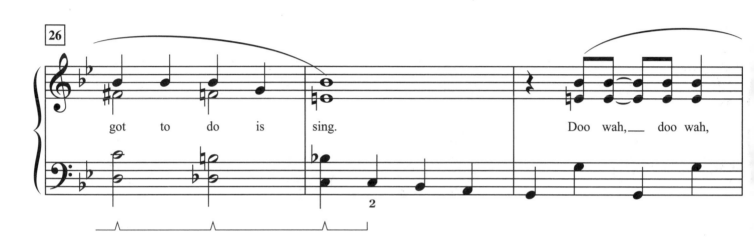

got to do is sing. Doo wah,___ doo wah,

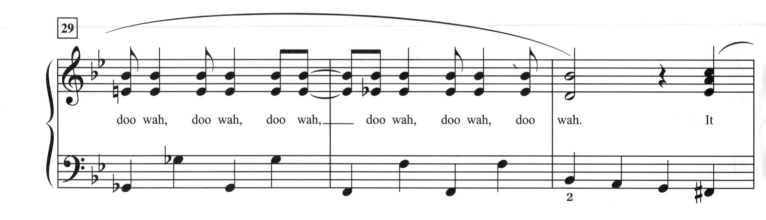

doo wah, doo wah, doo wah,___ doo wah, doo wah, doo wah. It

makes no diff-'rence if it's sweet or hot.___

MOONLIGHT SERENADE

Music by Glenn Miller
Arranged by Bernadine Johnson

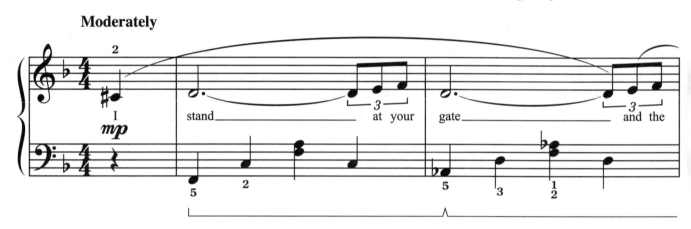

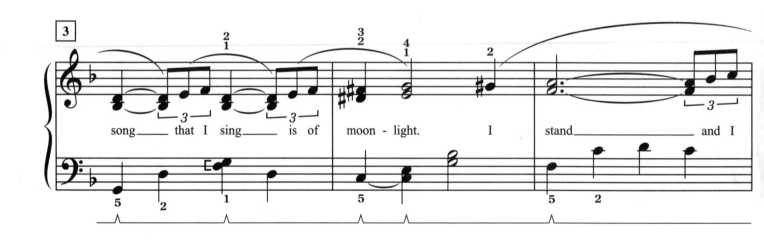

16

bring you   and   sing you   a   moon - light   ser - e -

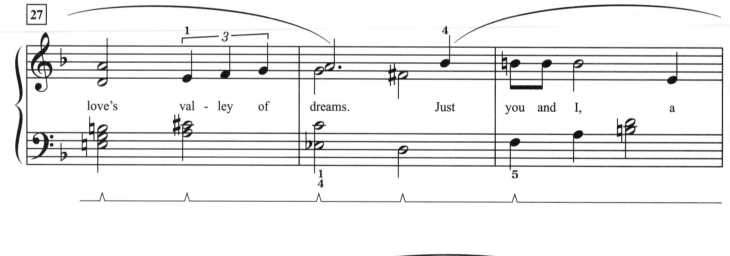

nade.   Let us stray   till   break of day   in

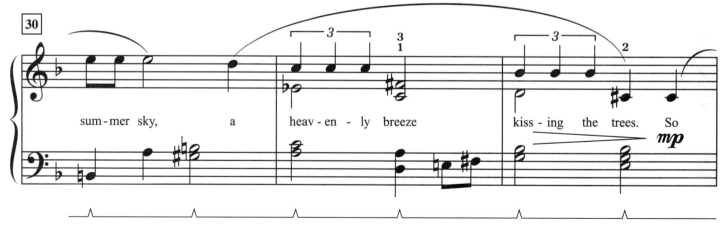

love's   val - ley of   dreams.   Just   you and I,   a

sum - mer sky,   a   heav - en - ly breeze   kiss - ing the trees. So

MOONGLOW

Words and Music by
Will Hudson, Eddie Delange and Irving Mills
Arranged by Bernadine Johnson

Moderate swing

mf

It must have been

moon - glow

way up in the blue.

It must have been moon - glow

that___ led me

straight to you.

I still hear you say - ing,

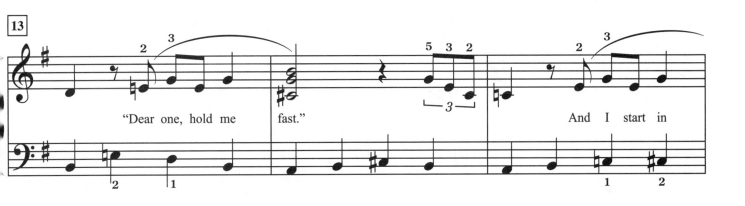

"Dear one, hold me fast." And I start in

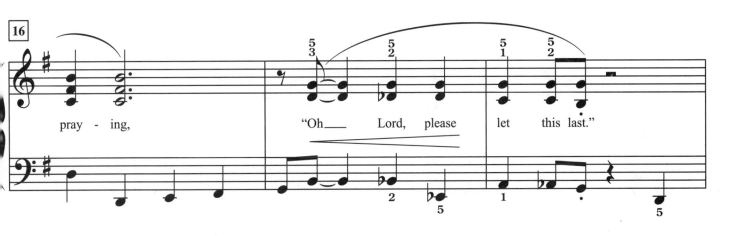

pray - ing, "Oh____ Lord, please let this last."

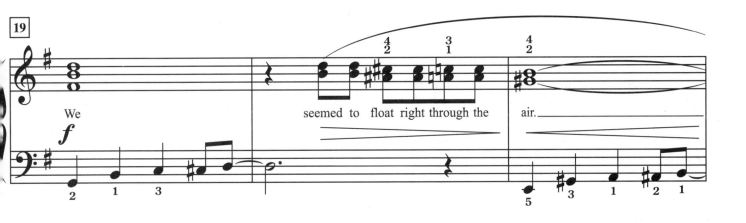

We seemed to float right through the air.____

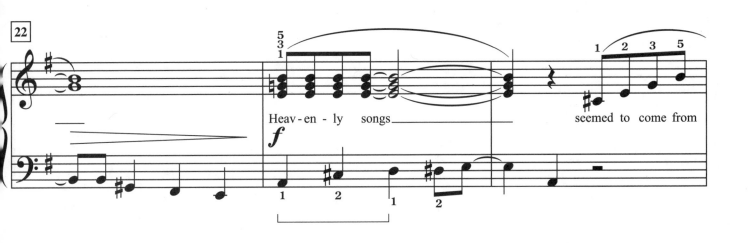

Heav - en - ly songs____ seemed to come from

ev - 'ry - where.
And now when there's
mf

moon - glow
way up in the blue

I al - ways re - mem - ber
that___ moon - glow

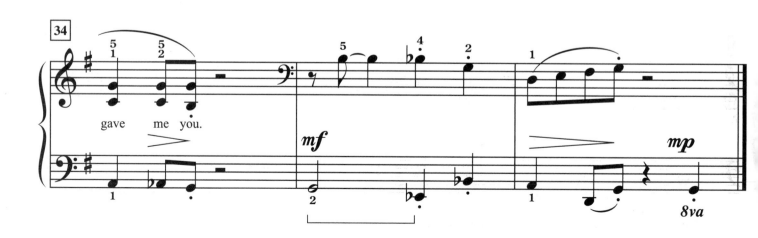

gave me you.
mf
mp
8va

MY FUNNY VALENTINE

Words by Lorenz Hart
Music by Richard Rodgers
Arranged by Bernadine Johnson

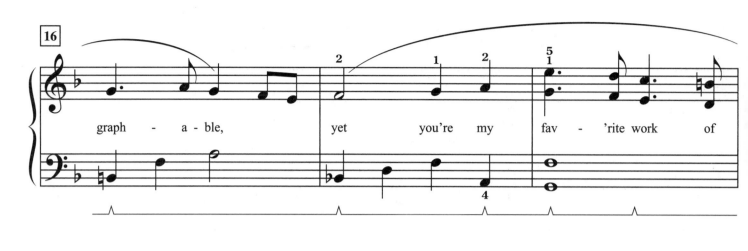

graph - a - ble, yet you're my fav - 'rite work of

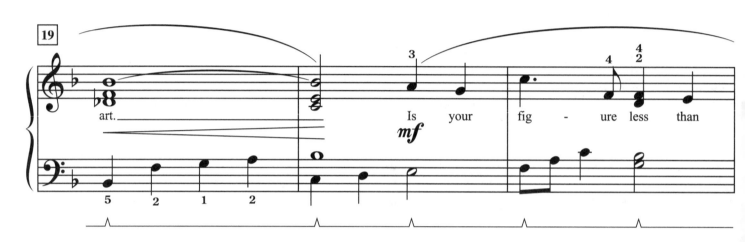

art. Is your fig - ure less than

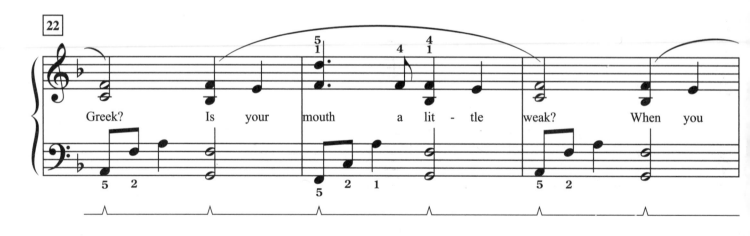

Greek? Is your mouth a lit - tle weak? When you

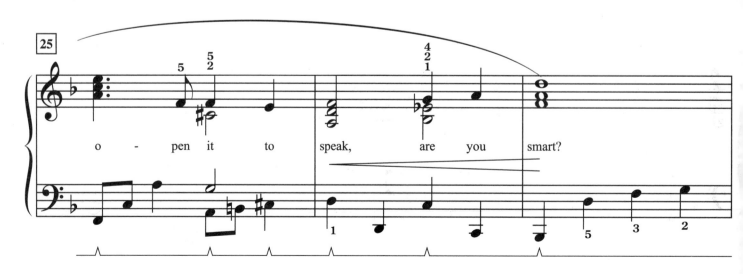

o - pen it to speak, are you smart?

STAR DUST

Music by Hoagy Carmichael
Words by Mitchell Parish
French Translation by Yvette Baruch
Arranged by Bernadine Johnson

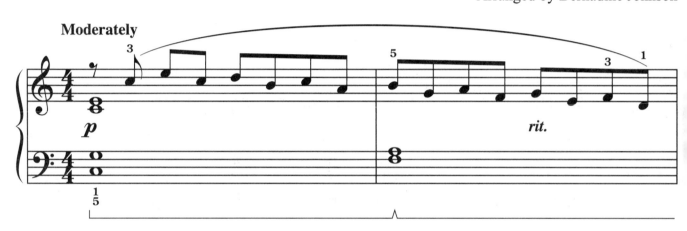

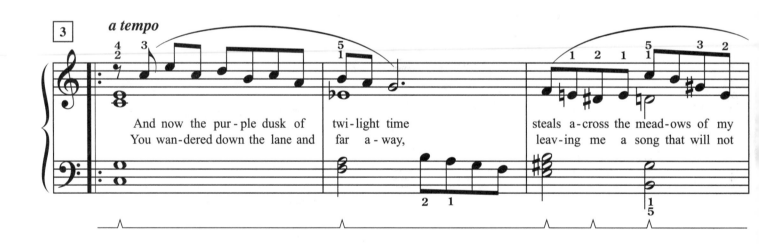

And now the pur - ple dusk of
You wan - dered down the lane and

twi - light time
far a - way,

steals a - cross the mead - ows of my
leav - ing me a song that will not

heart.
die.

High up in the sky the
Love is now the star dust

lit - tle stars climb,
of yes - ter - day,

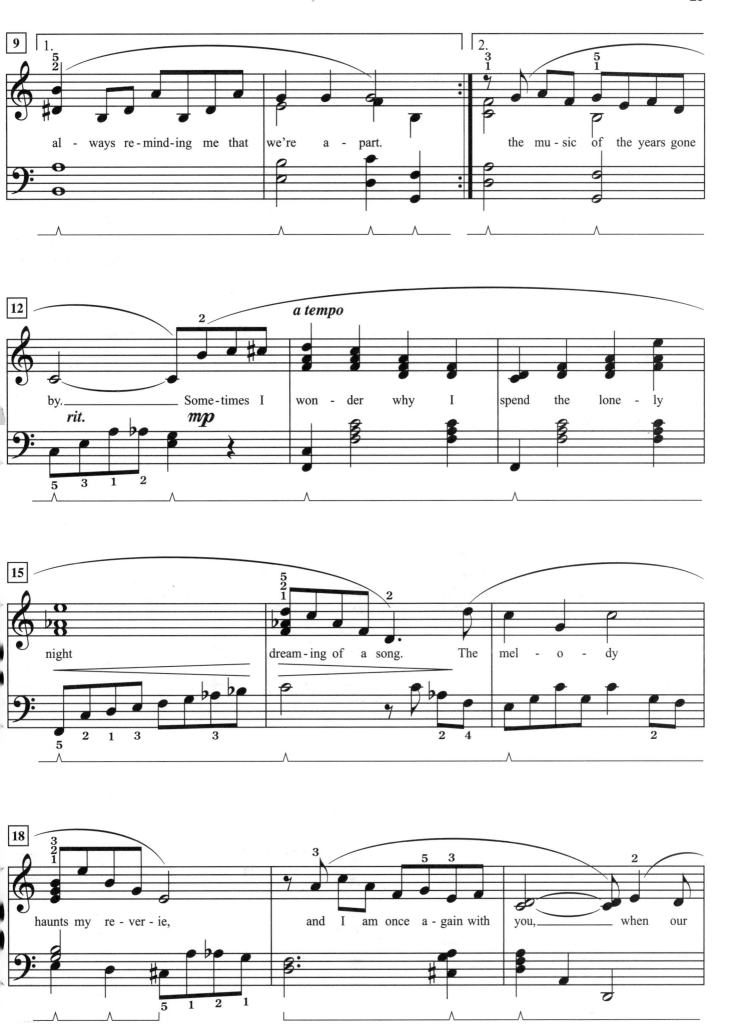

A STRING OF PEARLS

By Jerry Gray
Arranged by Bernadine Johnson

Moderately, with swing

Ba - by,____ here's
Ba - by,____ you

____ a   five and dime.   Ba - by,____ now's____ a - bout the time
____ made quite a start,   found   the____ way____ right   to   my heart

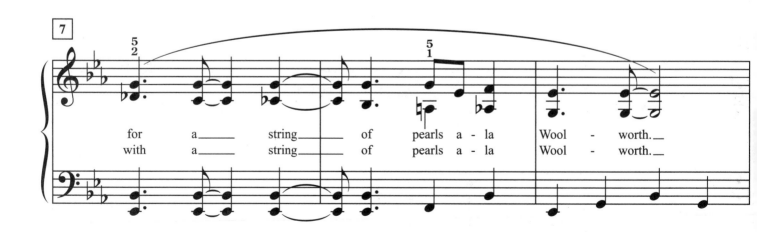

for   a____ string____ of pearls a - la Wool - worth.____
with   a____ string____ of pearls a - la Wool - worth.____

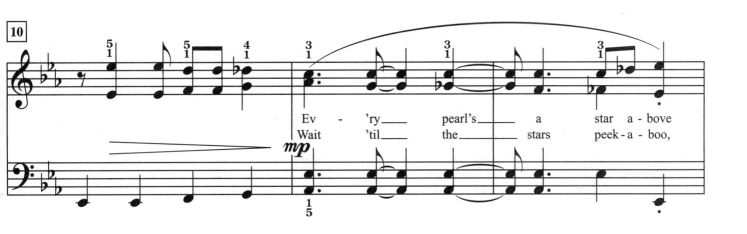

Ev - 'ry___ pearl's___ a star a - bove
Wait 'til___ the___ stars peek - a - boo,

wrapped in___ dreams___ and filled with love. That old___ string___
I've got___ some - thing just for you. It's a___ string___

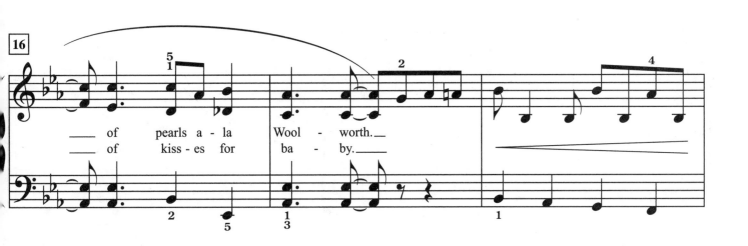

___ of pearls a - la Wool - worth.___
___ of kiss - es for ba - by.___

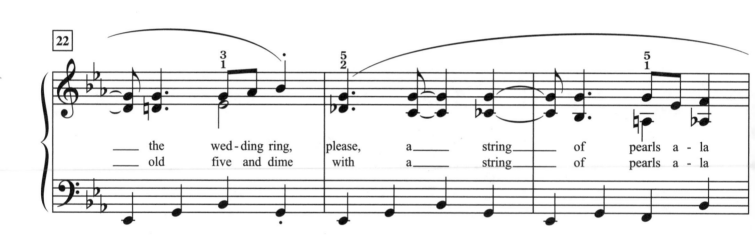

TAKE THE "A" TRAIN

Words and Music by Billy Strayhorn
Arranged by Bernadine Johnson

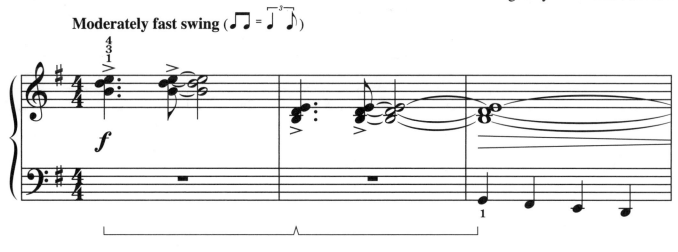

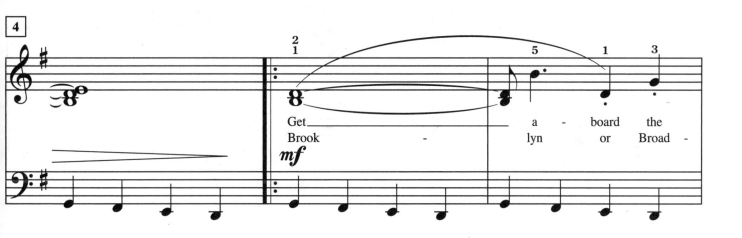

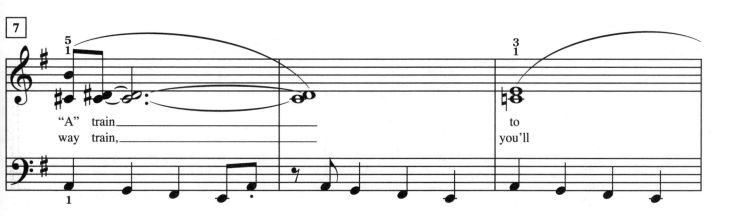

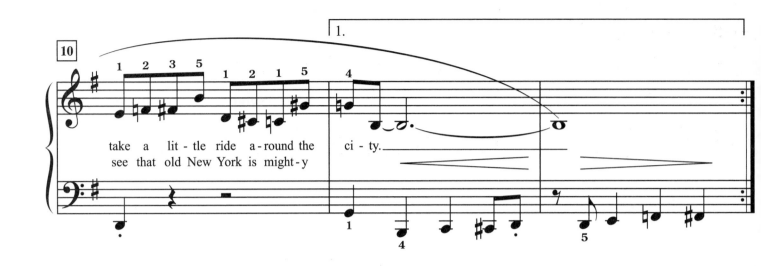

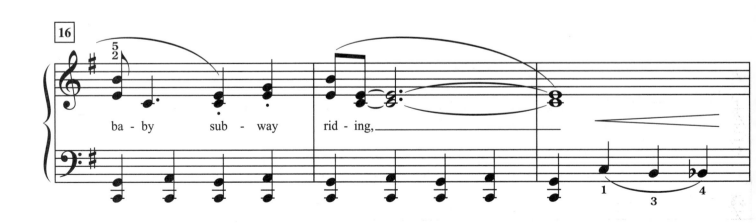

THEY CAN'T TAKE THAT AWAY FROM ME

Music and Lyrics by
George Gershwin and Ira Gershwin
Arranged by Bernadine Johnson

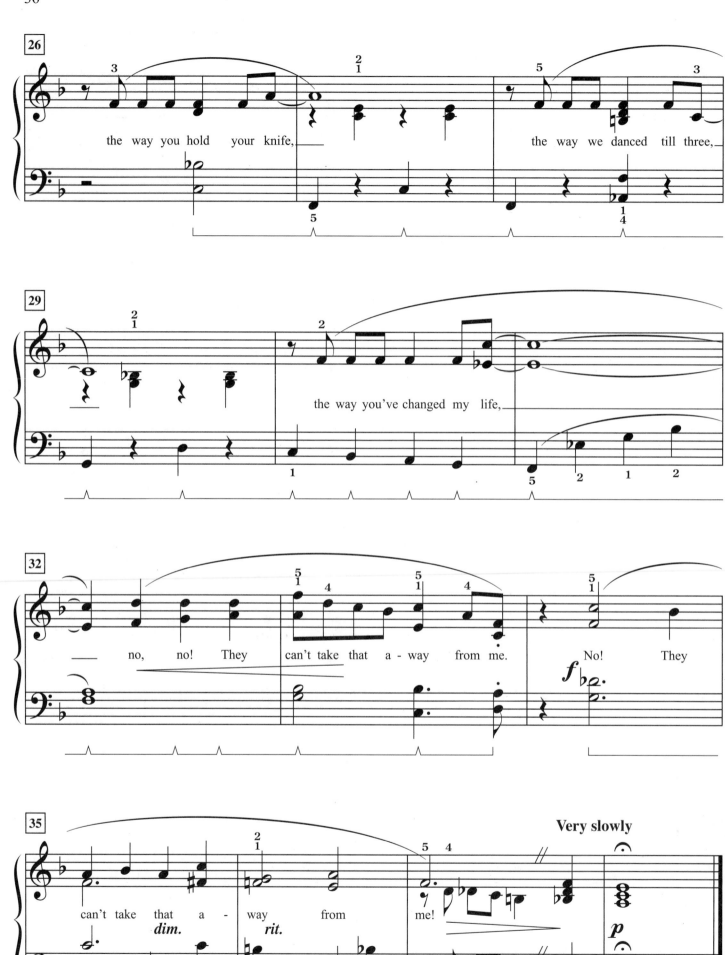